OSCAR WILDE

Selected Poems

BLOOMSBURY
★ POETRY ★
CLASSICS

This selection by Ian Hamilton first published 1995
Copyright © 1995 by Bloomsbury Publishing Plc

Bloomsbury Publishing Plc, 2 Soho Square,
London W1V 6HB

A CIP catalogue record for this book is available
from the British Library

ISBN 0 7475 2261 8

10 9 8 7 6 5 4 3 2 1

Typeset by Hewer Text Composition Services Limited,
Edinburgh
Printed in Great Britain by
HarperCollins Manufacturing, Glasgow
Jacket design by Jeff Fisher

CONTENTS

HÉLAS!

To drift with every passion till my soul
Is a stringed lute on which all winds can play,
Is it for this that I have given away
Mine ancient wisdom, and austere control?
Methinks my life is a twice-written scroll
Scrawled over on some boyish holiday
With idle songs for pipe and virelay,
Which do but mar the secret of the whole.
Surely there was a time I might have trod
The sunlit heights, and from life's dissonance
Struck one clear chord to reach the ears of God:
Is that time dead? lo! with a little rod
I did but touch the honey of romance—
And must I lose a soul's inheritance?

SONNET TO LIBERTY

Not that I love thy children, whose dull eyes
See nothing save their own unlovely woe,
Whose minds know nothing, nothing care to
    know,—
But that the roar of thy Democracies,
Thy reigns of Terror, thy great Anarchies,
Mirror my wildest passions like the sea
And give my rage a brother – ! Liberty!
For this sake only do thy dissonant cries
Delight my discreet soul, else might all kings
By bloody knout or treacherous cannonades
Rob nations of their rights inviolate
And I remain unmoved – and yet, and yet,
These Christs that die upon the barricades,
God knows it I am with them, in some things.

TO MILTON

Milton! I think thy spirit hath passed away
From these white cliffs and high-embattled towers;
This gorgeous fiery-coloured world of ours
Seems fallen into ashes dull and grey,
And the age changed unto a mimic play
Wherein we waste our else too-crowded hours:
For all our pomp and pageantry and powers
We are but fit to delve the common clay,
Seeing this little isle on which we stand,
This England, this sea-lion of the sea,
By ignorant demagogues is held in fee,
Who love her not: Dear God! is this the land
Which bare a triple empire in her hand
When Cromwell spake the word Democracy!

QUANTUM MUTATA

There was a time in Europe long ago
    When no man died for freedom anywhere,
      But England's lion leaping from its lair
Laid hands on the oppressor! it was so
    While England could a great Republic show.
      Witness the men of Piedmont, chiefest care
      Of Cromwell, when with impotent despair
The Pontiff in his painted portico
    Trembled before our stern ambassadors.
      How comes it then that from such high estate
      We have thus fallen, save that Luxury
    With barren merchandise piles up the gate
    Where noble thoughts and deeds should enter by:
      Else might we still be Milton's heritors.

LIBERTATIS SACRA FAMES

Albeit nurtured in democracy,
And liking best that state republican
　　Where every man is Kinglike and no man
　　Is crowned above his fellows, yet I see,
　　Spite of this modern fret for Liberty,
　　　　Better the rule of One, whom all obey,
　　　　Than to let clamorous demagogues betray
Our freedom with the kiss of anarchy.
Wherefore I love them not whose hands profane
　　Plant the red flag upon the piled-up street
　　For no right cause, beneath whose ignorant reign
Arts, Culture, Reverence, Honour, all things fade,
　　Save Treason and the dagger of her trade,
And Murder with his silent bloody feet.

THEORETIKOS

This mighty empire hath but feet of clay
  Of all its ancient chivalry and might
  Our little island is forsaken quite:
Some enemy hath stolen its crown of bay,
And from its hills that voice hath passed away
  Which spake of Freedom: O come out of it,
  Come out of it, my Soul, thou art not fit
  For this vile traffic-house, where day by day
  Wisdom and reverence are sold at mart,
  And the rude people rage with ignorant cries
Against an heritage of centuries.
  It mars my calm: wherefore in dreams of Art
  And loftiest culture I would stand apart,
Neither for God, nor for his enemies.

Spirit of Beauty, tarry yet awhile!
  Although the cheating merchants of the mart
With iron roads profane our lovely isle,
  And break on whirling wheels the limbs of Art,
Ay! though the crowded factories beget
The blind-worm Ignorance that slays the soul, O
    tarry yet!

For one at least is there,—He bears his name
  From Dante and the seraph Gabriel,—
Whose double laurels burn with deathless flame
  To light thine altar; He too loves thee well,
Who saw old Merlin lured in Vivien's snare,
And the white feet of angels coming down the
    golden stair,

Loves thee so well, that all the World for him
  A gorgeous-coloured vestiture must wear,
And Sorrow take a purple diadem,
  Or else be no more Sorrow, and Despair
Gild its own thorns, and Pain, like Adon, be
Even in anguish beautiful;—such is the empery

Which Painters hold, and such the heritage
  This gentle solemn Spirit doth possess,
Being a better mirror of his age
  In all his pity, love, and weariness,
Than those who can but copy common things,
And leave the Soul unpainted with its mighty
    questionings.

But they are few, and all romance has flown,
  And men can prophesy about the sun,
And lecture on his arrows—how, alone,
  Through a waste void the soulless atoms run,
How far from each tree its weeping nymph has fled,
And that no more 'mid English reeds a Naiad
    shows her head.

Methinks these new Actæons boast too soon
  That they have spied on beauty: what if we
Have analysed the rainbow, robbed the moon
  Of her most ancient, chastest mystery,
Shall I, the last Endymion, lose all hope
Because rude eyes peer at my mistress through a
    telescope!

What profit if this scientific age
    Burst though our gates with all its retinue
Of modern miracles! Can it assuage
    One lover's breaking heart? what can it do
To make one life more beautiful, one day
More godlike in its period? but now the age of Clay

Returns in horrid cycle, and the earth
    Hath borne again a noisy progeny
Of ignorant Titans, whose ungodly birth
    Hurls them against the august hierarchy
Which sat upon Olympus, to the Dust
They have appealed, and to that barren arbiter
        they must

Repair of judgment, let them, if they can,
    From Natural Warfare and insensate Chance,
Create the new Ideal rule for man!
    Methinks that was not my inheritance;
For I was nurtured otherwise, my soul
Passes from higher heights of life to a more supreme
        goal

Lo! while we spake the earth did turn away
   Her visage from the God, and Hecate's boat
Rose silver-laden, till the jealous day
   Blew all its torches out: I did not note
The waning hours, to young Endymions
Time's palsied fingers count in vain his rosary of
    suns!

Mark how the yellow iris wearily
   Leans back its throat, as though it would be
    kissed
By its false chamberer, the dragon-fly,
   Who, like a blue vein on a girl's white wrist,
Sleeps on that snowy primrose of the night,
Which 'gins to flush with crimson shame, and die
    beneath the light.

Come let us go, against the pallid shield
   Of the wan sky the almond blossoms gleam,
The corncrake nested in the unmown field
   Answers its mate, across the misty stream
On fitful wing the startled curlews fly,
And in his sedgy bed the lark, for joy that Day is
    nigh,

Scatters the pearlèd dew from off the grass,
   In tremulous ecstasy to greet the sun
Who soon in gilded panoply will pass
   Forth from yon orange-curtained pavilion
Hung in the burning east, see, the red rim
O'ertops the expectant hills! it is the God! for love
     of him

Already the shrill lark is out of sight,
   Flooding with waves of song this silent dell,—
Ah! there is something more in that bird's flight
   Than could be tested in a crucible!—
But the air freshens, let us go, why soon
The woodmen will be here; how we have lived this
     night of June!

REQUIESCAT

Tread lightly, she is near
    Under the snow,
Speak gently, she can hear
    The daisies grow.

All her bright golden hair
    Tarnished with rush,
She that was young and fair
    Fallen to dust.

Lily-like, white as snow,
    She hardly knew
She was a woman, so
    Sweetly she grew.

Coffin-board, heavy stone,
    Lie on her breast,
I vex my heart alone,
    She is at rest.

Peace, peace, she cannot hear
    Lyre or sonnet,
All my life's buried here,
    Heap earth upon it.

SONNET ON APPROACHING ITALY

I reached the Alps: the soul within me burned,
  Italia, my Italia, at thy name:
  And when from out the mountain's heart I came
And saw the land for which my life had yearned,
I laughed as one who some great prize had earned:
  And musing on the marvel of thy fame
  I watched the day, till marked with wounds of
      flame
The turquoise sky to burnished gold was turned.
The pine-trees waved as waves a woman's hair,
  And in the orchards every twining spray
  Was breaking into flakes of blossoming foam:
But when I knew that far away at Rome
  In evil bonds a second Peter lay,
  I wept to see the land so very fair.

SAN MINIATO

See, I have climbed the mountain side
Up to this holy house of God,
Where once that Angel-Painter trod
Who saw the heavens opened wide,

And throned upon the crescent moon
The Virginal white Queen of Grace,—
Mary! could I but see thy face
Death could not come at all too soon.

O crowned by God with thorns and pain!
Mother of Christ! O mystic wife!
My heart is weary of this life
And over-sad to sing again.

O crowned by God with love and flame!
O crowned by Christ the Holy One!
O listen ere the searching sun
Show to the world my sin and shame.

AVE MARIA GRATIA PLENA

Was this His coming! I had hoped to see
   A scene of wondrous glory, as was told
   Of some great God who in a rain of gold
Broke open bars and fell on Danae:
Or a dread vision as when Semele
   Sickening for love and unappeased desire
   Prayed to see God's clear body, and the fire
Caught her white limbs and slew her utterly:
With such glad dreams I sought this holy place,
   And now with wondering eyes and heart I stand
   Before this supreme mystery of Love:
A kneeling girl with passionless pale face,
   An angel with a lily in his hand,
   And over both with outstretched wings the
      Dove.

ITALIA

Italia! thou art fallen, though with sheen
  Of battle-spears thy clamorous armies stride
  From the north Alps to the Sicilian tide!
Ay! fallen, though the nations hail thee Queen
Because rich gold in every town is seen,
  And on thy sapphire-lake in tossing pride
  Of wind-filled vans thy myriad galleys ride
Beneath one flag of red and white and green.
O Fair and Strong! O Strong and Fair in vain!
  Look southward where Rome's desecrated town
  Lies mourning for her God-anointed King!
Look heaven-ward! shall God allow this thing?
  Nay! but some flame-girt Raphael shall come down,
  And smite the Spoiler with the sword of pain.

SONNET
Written in Holy Week at Genoa

I wandered in Scoglietto's green retreat,
   The oranges on each o'erhanging spray
   Burned as bright lamps of gold to shame the day;
Some startled bird with fluttering wings and fleet
Made snow of all the blossoms, at my feet
   Like silver moons the pale narcissi lay:
   And the curved waves that streaked the sapphire
     bay
Laughed i' the sun, and life seemed very sweet.
Outside the young boy-priest passed singing clear,
   'Jesus the son of Mary has been slain,
   O come and fill his sepulchre with flowers.'
Ah, God! Ah, God! those dear Hellenic hours
   Had drowned all memory of Thy bitter pain,
   The Cross, the Crown, the Soldiers and the
     Spear.

URBS SACRA ÆTERNA

Rome! what a scroll of History thine has been;
  In the first days thy sword republican
  Ruled the whole world for many an age's span:
Then of the peoples thou wert crownéd Queen,
Till in thy streets the bearded Goth was seen:
  And now upon thy walls the breezes fan
  (Ah, city crowned by God, discrowned by man!)
The hated flag of red and white and green.
When was thy glory! when in search for power
  Thine eagles flew to greet the double sun,
  And all the nations trembled at thy rod?
Nay, but thy glory tarried for this hour,
  When pilgrims kneel before the Holy One,
  The prisoned shepherd of the Church of God.

SONNET

On Hearing the Dies Iræ Sung in the Sistine Chapel

Nay, Lord, not thus! white lilies in the spring,
   Sad olive-groves, or silver-breasted dove,
   Teach me more clearly of Thy life and love
Than terrors of red flame and thundering.
The empurpled vines dear memories of Thee bring:
   A bird at evening flying to its nest
   Tells me of One who had no place of rest:
I think it is of Thee the sparrows sing.
Come rather on some autumn afternoon,
   When red and brown are burnished on the
     leaves.
   And the fields echo to the gleaner's song,
Come when the splendid fulness of the moon
   Looks down upon the rows of golden shaves,
   And reap Thy harvest: we have waited long.

EASTER DAY

The silver trumpets rang across the Dome:
　　The people knelt upon the ground with awe:
　　And borne upon the necks of men I saw,
Like some great God, the Holy Lord of Rome.
Priest-like, he wore a robe more white than foam,
　　And, king-like, swathed himself in royal red,
　　Three crowns of gold rose high upon his head:
In splendour and in light the Pope passed home.
My heart stole back across wide wastes of years
　　To One who wandered by a lonely sea,
　　And sought in vain for any place of rest:
　　'Foxes have holes, and every bird its nest.
　　I, only I, must wander wearily,
　　And bruise my feet, and drink wine salt with tears.'

VITA NUOVA

I stood by the unvintageable sea
   Till the wet waves drenched face and hair with
      spray;
   The long red fires of the dying day
Burned in the west, the wind piped drearily;
And to the land the clamorous gulls did flee:
   'Alas!' I cried, 'my life is full of pain,
   And who can garner fruit or golden grain
From these waste fields which travel ceaselessly!'
My nets gaped wide with many a break and flaw,
   Nathless I threw them as my final cast
   Into the sea, and waited for the end.
When lo! a sudden glory! and I saw
   The argent splendour of white limbs ascend,
   And in that joy forgot my tortured past.

MADONNA MIA

A lily-girl, not made for this world's pain,
　　With brown, soft hair close braided by her ears,
　　And longing eyes half veiled by slumberous tears
Like bluest water seen through mists of rain:
Pale cheeks whereon no love hath left its stain,
　　Red underlip drawn in for fear of love,
　　And white throat, whiter than the silvered dove,
Through whose wan marble creeps one purple vein.
Yet, though my lips shall praise her without cease,
　　Even to kiss her feet I am not bold,
　　Being o'ershadowed by the wings of awe,
Like Dante, when he stood with Beatrice
　　Beneath the flaming Lion's breast, and saw
　　The seventh Crystal, and the Stair of Gold.

FROM THE BURDEN OF ITYS

Sing on! sing on! I would be drunk with life,
  Drunk with the trampled vintage of my youth.
I would forget the wearying wasted strife,
  The riven veil, the Gorgon eyes of Truth,
The prayerless vigil and the cry for prayer,
The barren gifts, the lifted arms, the dull insensate
    air!

Sing on! sing on! O feathered Niobe,
  Thou canst make sorrow beautiful, and steal
From joy its sweetest music, not as we
  Who by dead voiceless silence strive to heal
Our too untented wounds, and do but keep
Pain barricadoed in our hearts, and murder
    pillowed sleep.

Sing louder yet, why must I still behold
  The wan white face of that deserted Christ,
Whose bleeding hands my hands did once enfold,
  Whose smitten lips my lips so oft have kissed,
And now in mute and marble misery
Sits in his lone dishonoured House and weeps,
    perchance for me?

IMPRESSION DU MATIN

The Thames nocturne of blue and gold
   Changed to a Harmony in grey:
   A barge with ochre-coloured hay
Dropt from the wharf: and chill and cold

The yellow fog came creeping down
   The bridges, till the houses' walls
   Seemed changed to shadows and St Paul's
Loomed like a bubble o'er the town.

Then suddenly arose the clang
   Of waking life; the streets were stirred
   With country waggons: and a bird
Flew to the glistening roofs and sang.

But one pale woman all alone,
   The daylight kissing her wan hair,
   Loitered beneath the gas lamps' flare,
With lips of flame and heart of stone.

ATHANASIA

To that gaunt House of Art which lacks for naught
  Of all the great things men have saved from Time,
The withered body of a girl was brought
  Dead ere the world's glad youth had touched its
    prime,
And seen by lonely Arabs lying hid
In the dim womb of some black pyramid.

But when they had unloosed the linen band
  Which swathed the Egyptian's body, – lo! was
    found
Closed in the wasted hollow of her hand
  A little seed, which sown in English ground
Did wondrous snow of starry blossoms bear
And spread rich odours through our spring-tide air.

With such strange arts this flower did allure
  That all forgotten was the asphodel,
And the brown bee, the lily's paramour,
  Forsook the cup where he was wont to dwell,
For not a thing of earth it seemed to be,
But stolen from some heavenly Arcady.

In vain the sad narcissus, wan and white
    At its own beauty, hung across the stream,
The purple dragon-fly had no delight
    With its gold dust to make his wings a-gleam,
Ah! no delight the jasmine-bloom to kiss,
Or brush the rain-pearls from the eucharis.

For love of it the passionate nightingale
    Forgot the hills of Thrace, the cruel king,
And the pale dove no longer cared to sail
    Through the wet woods at time of blossoming,
But round this flower of Egypt sought to float,
With silvered wing and amethystine throat.

While the hot sun blazed in his tower of blue
    A cooling wind crept from the land of snows,
And the warm south with tender tears of dew
    Drenched its white leaves when Herperos up-rose
Amid those sea-green meadows of the sky
On which the scarlet bars of sunset lie.

But when o'er wastes of lily-haunted field
    The tired birds had stayed their amorous tune,
And broad and glittering like an argent shield
    High in the sapphire heavens hung the moon,
Did no strange dream or evil memory make
Each tremulous petal of its blossoms shake?

Ah no! to this bright flower a thousand years
  Seemed but the lingering of a summer's day,
It never knew the tide of cankering fears
  Which turn a boy's gold hair to withered grey,
The dread desire of death it never knew,
Or how all folk that they were born must rue.

For we to death with pipe and dancing go,
  Now would we pass the ivory gate again,
As some sad river wearied of its flow
  Through the dull plains, the haunts of common
    men,
Leaps lover-like into the terrible sea!
And counts it gain to die so gloriously.

We mar our lordly strength in barren strife
  With the world's legions led by clamorous care,
It never feels decay but gathers life
  From the pure sunlight and the supreme air,
We live beneath Time's wasting sovereignty,
It is the child of all eternity.

SERENADE
(For Music)

The western wind is blowing fair
   Across the dark Ægean sea,
And at the secret marble stair
   My Tyrian galley waits for thee.
Come down! the purple sail is spread,
   The watchman sleeps within the town,
O leave thy lily-flowered bed,
   O Lady mine come down, come down!

She will not come, I know her well,
   Of lover's vows she hath no care,
And little good a man can tell
   Of one so cruel and so fair.
True love is but a woman's toy,
   They never know the lover's pain,
And I who loved as loves a boy
   Must love in vain, must love in vain.

O noble pilot, tell me true,
   Is that the sheen of golden hair?
Or is it but the tangled dew
   That binds the passion-flowers there?
Good sailor come and tell me now
   Is that my Lady's lily hand?
Or is it but the gleaming prow,
   Or is it but the silver sand?

No! no! 'tis not the tangled dew,
   'Tis not the silver-fretted sand,
It is my own dear Lady true
   With golden hair and lily hand!
O noble pilot, steer for Troy,
   Good sailor, ply the labouring oar,
This is the Queen of life and joy
   Whom we must bear from Grecian shore!

The waning sky grows faint and blue,
   It wants an hour still of day,
Aboard! aboard! my gallant crew,
   O Lady mine, away! away!
O noble pilot, steer for Troy,
   Good sailor, ply the labouring oar,
O loved as only loves a boy!
   O loved for ever evermore!

ENDYMION
(For Music)

The apple trees are hung with gold,
  And birds are loud in Arcady,
The sheep lie bleating in the fold,
The wild goat runs across the wold,
But yesterday his love he told,
  I know he will come back to me.
O rising moon! O Lady moon!
  Be you my lover's sentinel,
  You cannot choose but know him well,
For he is shod with purple shoon,
You cannot choose but know my love,
  For he a shepherd's crook doth bear,
And he is soft as any dove,
  And brown and curly is his hair.

The turtle now has ceased to call
  Upon her crimson-footed groom,
The grey wolf prowls about the stall,
The lily's singing seneschal
Sleeps in the lily-bell, and all
  The violet hills are lost in gloom.
O risen moon! O holy moon!
  Stand on the top of Helice.
  And if my own true love you see,
Ah! if you see the purple shoon,
The hazel crook, the lad's brown hair,

The goat-skin wrapped about his arm,
Tell him that I am waiting where
    The rushlight glimmers in the Farm.

The falling dew is cold and chill,
    And no bird sings in Arcady,
The little fauns have left the hill,
Even the tired daffodil
Has closed its gilded doors, and still
    My lover comes not back to me.
False moon! False moon! O waning moon!
    Where is my own true lover gone,
    Where are the lips vermilion,
The shepherd's crook, the purple shoon?
Why spread that silver pavilion,
    Why wear that veil of drifting mist?
Ah! thou hast young Endymion,
    Thou hast the lips that should be kissed!

LA BELLA DONNA DELLA MIA MENTE

My limbs are wasted with a flame,
  My feet are sore with travelling,
For, calling on my Lady's name,
  My lips have now forgot to sing.

O Linnet in the wild-rose brake
  Strain for my Love thy melody,
O Lark sing louder for love's sake,
  My gentle Lady passeth by.

She is too fair for any man
  To see or hold his heart's delight,
Fairer than Queen or courtesan
  Or moonlit water in the night.

Her hair is bound with myrtle leaves,
  (Green leaves upon her golden hair!)
Green grasses through the yellow sheaves
  Of autumn corn are not more fair.

Her little lips, more made to kiss
  Than to cry bitterly for pain,
Are tremulous as brook-water is,
  Or roses after evening rain.

Her neck is like white melilote
   Flushing for pleasure of the sun,
The throbbing of the linnet's throat
   Is not so sweet to look upon.

As a pomegranate, cut in twain,
   White-seeded, in her crimson mouth,
Her cheeks are as the fading stain
   Where the peach reddens to the south.

O twining hands! O delicate
   White body made for love and pain!
O House of love! O desolate
   Pale flower beaten by the rain!

FROM CHARMIDES

1

He was a Grecian lad, who coming home
  With pulpy figs and wine from Sicily
Stood at his galley's prow, and let the foam
  Blow through his crisp brown curls unconsciously,
And holding wave and wind in boy's despite
Peered from his dripping seat across the wet and
    stormy night.

Till with the dawn he saw a burnished spear
  Like a thin thread of gold against the sky,
And hoisted sail, and strained the creaking gear,
  And bade the pilot head her lustily
Against the nor-west gale, and all day long
Held on his way, and marked the rowers' time with
    measured song,

And when the faint Corinthian hills were red
  Dropped anchor in a little sandy bay,
And with fresh boughs of olive crowned his head,
  And brushed from cheek and throat the hoary
    spray,
And washed his limbs with oil, and from the hold
Brought his linen tunic and his sandals brazen-soled,

And a rich robe stained with the fishes' juice
  Which of some swarthy trader he had bought
Upon the sunny quay at Syracuse,
  And was with Tyrian broideries inwrought,
And by the questioning merchants made his way
Up through the soft and silver woods, and when the
    labouring day

Had spun its tangled web of crimson cloud,
  Clomb the high hill, and with swift silent feet
Crept to the fane unnoticed by the crowd
  Of busy priests, and from some dark retreat
Watched the young swains his frolic playmates bring
The firstling of their little flock, and the shy
    shepherd fling

The crackling salt upon the flame, or hang
  His studded crook against the temple wall
To Her who keeps away the ravenous fang
  Of the base wolf from homestead and from stall;
And then the clear-voiced maidens 'gan to sing,
  And to the altar each man brought some goodly
    offering,

A beechen cup brimming with milky foam,
  A fair cloth wrought with cunning imagery
Of hounds in chase, a waxen honey-comb
  Dripping with oozy gold which scarce the bee
Had ceased from building, a black skin of oil
Meet for the wrestlers, a great boar the fierce and
    white-tusked spoil

Stolen from Artemis that jealous maid
  To please Athena, and the dappled hide
Of a tall stag who in some mountain glade
  Had met the shaft; and then the herald cried,
And from the pillared precinct one by one
Went the glad Greeks well pleased that they their
    simple vows had done.

And the old priest put out the waning fires
  Save that one lamp whose restless ruby glowed
For ever in the cell, and the shrill lyres
  Came fainter on the wind, as down the road
In joyous dance these country folk did pass,
And with stout hands the warder closed the gates of
    polished brass.

Long time he lay and hardly dared to breathe,
    And heard the cadenced drip of spilt-out wine,
And the rose-petals falling from the wreath
    As the night breezes wandered through the shrine,
And seemed to be in some entranced swoon
Till through the open roof above the full and
        brimming moon

Flooded with sheeny waves the marble floor,
    When from his nook up leapt the venturous lad,
And flinging wide the cedar-carven door
    Beheld an awful image saffron-clad
And armed for battle! the gaunt Griffin glared
From the huge helm, and the long lance of wreck
        and ruin flared

Like a red rod of flame, stony and steeled,
    The Gorgon's head its leaden eyeballs rolled,
And writhed its snaky horrors through the shield,
    And gaped aghast with bloodless lips and cold
In passion impotent, while with blind gaze
The blinking owl between the feet hooted in shrill
        amaze.

The lonely fisher as he trimmed his lamp
   Far out at sea off Sunium, or cast
The net for tunnies, heard a brazen tramp
   Of horses smite the waves, and a wild blast
Divide the folded curtains of the night,
And knelt upon the little poop, and prayed in holy
     fright.

And guilty lovers in their venery
   Forgat a little while their stolen sweets,
Deeming they heard dread Dian's bitter cry;
   And the grim watchmen on their lofty seats
Ran to their shields in haste precipitate,
Or strained black-bearded throats across the dusky
     parapet.

For round the temple rolled the clang of arms,
   And the twelve Gods leapt up in marble fear,
And the air quaked with dissonant alarums
   Till huge Poseidon shook his mighty spear,
And on the frieze the prancing horses neighed,
And the low tread of hurrying feet rang from the
     cavalcade.

Ready for death with parted lips he stood,
  And well content at such a price to see
That calm wide brow, that terrible maidenhood,
  The marvel of that pitiless chastity,
Ah! well content indeed, for never wight
Since Troy's young shepherd prince had seen so
    wonderful a sight.

Ready for death he stood, but lo! the air
  Grew silent, and the horses ceased to neigh,
And off his brow he tossed the clustering hair,
  And from his limbs he threw the cloak away;
For whom would not such love make desperate?
And nigher came, and touched her throat, and with
    hands violate

Undid the cuirass, and the crocus gown,
  And bared the breasts of polished ivory,
Till from the waist the peplos falling down
  Left visible the secret mystery
Which to no lover will Athena show,
The grand cool flanks, the crescent thighs, the bossy
    hills of snow.

Those who have never known a lover's sin
　　Let them not read my ditty, it will be
To their dull ears so musicless and thin
　　That they will have no joy of it, but ye
To whose wan cheeks now creeps the lingering smile,
Ye who have learned who Eros is, – O listen yet
　　　awhile.

A little space he let his greedy eyes
　　Rest on the burnished image, till mere sight
Half swooned for surfeit of such luxuries,
　　And then his lips in hungering delight
Fed on her lips, and round the towered neck
He flung his arms, nor cared at all his passion's will
　　　to check.

Never I ween did lover hold such tryst,
　　For all night long he murmured honeyed word,
And saw her sweet unravished limbs, and kissed
　　Her pale and argent body undisturbed,
And paddled with the polished throat, and pressed
His hot and beating heart upon her chill and icy
　　　breast.

It was as if Numidian javelins
  Pierced through and through his wild and whirling
    brain,
And his nerves thrilled like throbbing violins
  In exquisite pulsation, and the pain
Was such sweet anguish that he never drew
His lips from hers till overhead the lark of warning
    flew.

They who have never seen the daylight peer
  Into a darkened room, and drawn the curtain,
And with dull eyes and wearied from some dear
  And worshipped body risen, they for certain
Will never know of what I try to sing,
How long the last kiss was, how fond and late his
    lingering.

The moon was girdled with a crystal rim,
  The sign which shipmen say is ominous
Of wrath in heaven, the wan stars were dim
  And the low lightening east was tremulous
With the faint fluttering wings of flying dawn
Ere from the silent sombre shrine his lover had
    withdrawn.

Down the steep rock with hurried feet and fast
  Clomb the brave lad, and reached the cave of Pan,
And heard the goat-foot snoring as he passed,
  And leapt upon a grassy knoll and ran
Like a young fawn unto an olive wood
Which in a shady valley by the well-built city stood;

And sought a little stream, which well he knew,
  For oftentimes with boyish careless shout
The green and crested grebe he would pursue,
  Or snare in woven net the silver trout,
And down amid the startled reeds he lay
Panting in breathless sweet affright, and waited for
    the day.

On the green bank he lay, and let one hand
  Dip in the cool dark eddies listlessly,
And soon the breath of morning came and fanned
  His hot flushed cheeks, or lifted wantonly
The tangled curls from off his forehead, while
He on the running water gazed with strange and
    secret smile.

And soon the shepherd in rough woollen cloak
　　With his long crook undid the wattled cotes,
And from the stack a thin blue wreath of smoke
　　Curled through the air across the ripening oats,
And on the hill the yellow house-dog bayed
As through the crisp and rustling fern the heavy
　　　　cattle strayed.

And when the light-foot mower went afield
　　Across the meadows laced with threaded dew,
And the sheep bleated on the misty weald,
　　And from its nest the waking corncrake flew,
Some woodmen saw him lying by the stream
And marvelled much that any lad so beautiful could
　　　　seem,

Nor deemed him, born of mortals, and one said,
　　'It is young Hylas, that false runaway
Who with a Naiad now would make his bed
　　Forgetting Herakles,' but others, 'Nay,
It is Narcissus, his own paramour,
Those are the fond and crimson lips no woman can
　　　　allure.'

And when they nearer came a third one cried,
   'It is young Dionysos who has hid
His spear and fawnskin by the river side
   Weary of hunting with the Bassarid,
And wise indeed were we away to fly:
They live not long who on the gods immortal come
     to spy.'

So turned they back, and feared to look behind,
   And told the timid swain how they had seen
Amid the reeds some woodland God reclined,
   And no man dared to cross the open green,
And on that day no olive-tree was slain,
Nor rushes cut, but all deserted was the fair domain,

Save when the neat-herd's lad, his empty pail
   Well slung upon his back, with leap and bound
Raced on the other side, and stopped to hail,
   Hoping that he some comrade new had found,
And got no answer, and then half afraid
Passed on his simple way, or down the still and silent
     glade

A little girl ran laughing from the farm,
    Not thinking of love's secret mysteries,
And when she saw the white and gleaming arm
    And all his manlihood, with longing eyes
Whose passion mocked her sweet virginity
Watched him awhile, and then stole back sadly and
        wearily.

Far off he heard the city's hum and noise,
    And now and then the shriller laughter where
The passionate purity of brown-limbed boys
    Wrestled or raced in the clear healthful air,
And now and then a little tinkling bell
As the shorn wether led the sheep down to the
        mossy well.

Through the grey willows danced the fretful gnat,
    The grasshopper chirped idly from the tree,
In sleek and oily coat the water-rat
    Breasting the little ripples manfully
Made for the wild-duck's nest, from bough to bough
Hopped the shy finch, and the huge tortoise crept
        across the slough.

On the faint wind floated the silky seeds
   As the bright scythe swept through the waving
      grass,
The ousel-cock splashed circles in the reeds
   And flecked with silver whorls the forest's glass,
Which scarce had caught again its imagery
Ere from its bed the dusky tench leapt at the dragon-fly.

But little care had he for any thing
   Though up and down the beech the squirrel
      played,
And from the copse the linnet 'gan to sing
   To her brown mate her sweetest serenade;
Ah! little care indeed, for he had seen
The breasts of Pallas and the naked wonder of the
      Queen.

But when the herdsman called his straggling goats
   With whistling pipe across the rocky road,
And the shard-beetle with its trumpet-notes
   Boomed through the darkening woods, and
      seemed to bode
Of coming storm, and the belated crane
Passed homeward like a shadow, and the dull big
      drops of rain

Fell on the pattering fig-leaves, up he rose,
  And from the gloomy forest went his way
Past sombre homestead and wet orchard-close,
  And came at last unto a little quay,
And called his mates aboard, and took his seat
On the high poop, and pushed from land, and
    loosed the dripping sheet,

And steered across the bay, and when nine suns
  Passed down the long and laddered way of gold,
And nine pale moons had breathed their orisons
  To the chaste stars their confessors, or told
Their dearest secret to the downy moth
That will not fly at noonday, through the foam and
    surging froth

Came a great owl with yellow sulphurous eyes
  And lit upon the ship, whose timbers creaked
As though the lading of three argosies
  Were in the hold, and flapped its wings and
    shrieked,
And darkness straightway stole across the deep,
Sheathed was Orion's sword, dread Mars himself fled
    down the steep,

And the moon hid behind a tawny mask
  Of drifting cloud, and from the ocean's marge
Rose the red plume, the huge and hornèd casque,
  The seven-cubit spear, the brazen targe!
And clad in bright and burnished panoply
Athena strode across the stretch of sick and
      shivering sea!

To the dull sailors' sight her loosened locks
  Seemed like the jagged storm-rack, and her feet
Only the spume that floats on hidden rocks,
  And, marking how the rising waters beat
Against the rolling ship, the pilot cried
To the young helmsman at the stern to luff to
      windward side.

But he, the overbold adulterer,
  A dear profaner of great mysteries,
An ardent amorous idolater,
  When he beheld those grand relentless eyes
Laughed loud for joy, and crying out 'I come'
Leapt from the lofty poop into the chill and
      churning foam.

Then fell from the high heaven one bright star,
   One dancer left the circling galaxy,
And back to Athens on her clattering car
   In all the pride of venged divinity
Pale Pallas swept with shrill and steely clank,
And a few gurgling bubbles rose where her boy lover
      sank.

And the mast shuddered as the gaunt owl flew
   With mocking hoots after the wrathful Queen,
And the old pilot bade the trembling crew
   Hoist the big sail, and told how he had seen
Close to the stern a dim and giant form,
And like a dipping swallow the stout ship dashed
      through the storm.

And no man dared to speak of Charmides
   Deeming that he some evil thing had wrought,
And when they reached the strait Symplegades
   They beached their galley on the shore, and
      sought
The toll-gate of the city hastily,
And in the market showed their brown and pictured
      pottery.

LES SILHOUETTES

The sea is flecked with bars of grey,
The dull dead wind is out of tune,
And like a withered leaf the moon
Is blown across the stormy bay.

Etched clear upon the pallid sand
The black boat lies: a sailor boy
Clambers aboard in careless joy
With laughing face and gleaming hand.

And overhead the curlews cry,
Where through the dusky upland grass
The young brown-throated reapers pass,
Like silhouettes against the sky.

SANTA DECCA

The Gods are dead: no longer do we bring
   To grey-eyed Pallas crowns of olive-leaves!
   Demeter's child no more hath tithe of sheaves,
And in the noon the careless shepherds sing,
For Pan is dead, and all the wantoning
   By secret glade and devious haunt is o'er:
   Young Hylas seeks the water-springs no more;
Great Pan is dead, and Mary's son is King.

And yet – perchance in this sea-trancèd isle,
   Chewing the bitter fruit of memory,
   Some God lies hidden in the asphodel.
Ah Love! if such there be, then it were well
   For us to fly his anger: nay, but see,
   The leaves are stirring: let us watch awhile.

THE GRAVE OF SHELLEY

Like burnt-out torches by a sick man's bed
  Gaunt cypress-trees stand round the sun bleached
    stone;
  Here doth the little night-owl make her throne,
And the slight lizard show his jewelled head.
And, where the chaliced poppies flame to red,
  In the still chamber of yon pyramid
  Surely some Old-World Sphinx lurks darkly hid,
Grim warder of this pleasaunce of the dead.

Ah! sweet indeed to rest within the womb
  Of Earth, great mother of eternal sleep,
But sweeter far for thee a restless tomb
  In the blue cavern of an echoing deep,
Or where the tall ships founder in the gloom
  Against the rocks of some wave-shattered steep.

FROM PANTHEA

Nay, let us walk from fire unto fire,
   From passionate pain to deadlier delight,—
I am too young to live without desire,
   Too young art thou to waste this summer night
Asking those idle questions which of old
Man sought of seer and oracle, and no reply was told.

For, sweet, to feel is better than to know,
   And wisdom is a childless heritage,
One pulse of passion – youth's first fiery glow,—
   Are worth the hoarded proverbs of the sage:
Vex not thy soul with dead philosophy,
Have we not lips to kiss with, hearts to love and eyes
    to see!

Dost thou not hear the murmuring nightingale,
   Like water bubbling from a silver jar,
So soft she sings the envious moon is pale,
   That high in heaven she is hung so far
She cannot hear that love-enraptured tune,—
Mark how she wreathes each horn with mist, yon late
    and labouring moon.

White lilies, in whose cups the gold bees dream,
  The fallen snow of petals where the breeze
Scatters the chestnut blossom, or the gleam
  Of boyish limbs in water, – are not these
Enough for thee, dost thou desire more?
Alas! the Gods will give nought else from their eternal
    store.

For our high Gods have sick and wearied grown
  Of all our endless sins, our vain endeavour
For wasted days of youth to make atone
  By pain or prayer or priest, and never, never,
Hearken they now to either good or ill,
But send their rain upon the just and the unjust at
    will.

They sit at ease, our Gods they sit at ease,
  Strewing with leaves of rose their scented wine,
They sleep, they sleep, beneath the rocking trees
  Where asphodel and yellow lotus twine,
Mourning the old glad days before they knew
What evil things the heart of man could dream, and
    dreaming do.

And far beneath the brazen floor they see
   Like swarming flies the crowd of little men,
The bustle of small lives, then wearily
   Back to their lotus-haunts they turn again
Kissing each others' mouths, and mix more deep
The poppy-seeded draught which brings soft purple-
    lidded sleep.

HER VOICE

The wild bee reels from bough to bough
 With his furry coat and his gauzy wing,
Now in a lily-cup, and now
 Setting a jacinth bell a-swing,
  In his wandering;
Sit closer love: it was here I trow
  I made that vow,

Swore that two lives should be like one
 As long as the sea-gull loved the sea,
As long as the sunflower sought the sun,—
 It shall be, I said, for eternity
  'Twixt you and me!
Dear friend, those times are over and done;
  Love's web is spun.

Look upward where the poplar trees
 Sway and sway in the summer air,
Here in the valley never a breeze
 Scatters the thistledown, but there
  Great winds blow fair
From the mighty murmuring mystical seas,
  And the wave-lashed leas.

Look upward where the white gull screams,
　　What does it see that we do not see?
Is that a star? or the lamp that gleams
　　On some outward voyaging argosy,
　　　　Ah! can it be
We have lived our lives in a land of dreams!
　　How sad it seems.

Sweet, there is nothing left to say
　　But this, that love is never lost,
Keen winter stabs the breasts of May
　　Whose crimson roses burst his frost,
　　　　Ships tempest-tossed
Will find a harbour in some bay,
　　And so we may.

And there is nothing left to do
　　But to kiss once again, and part,
Nay, there is nothing we should rue,
　　I have my beauty, – you your Art,
　　　　Nay, do not start,
One world was not enough for two
　　Like me and you.

TÆDIUM VITÆ

To stab my youth with desperate knives, to wear
This paltry age's gaudy livery,
To let each base hand filch my treasury,
To mesh my soul within a woman's hair,
And be mere Fortune's lackeyed groom, – I swear
I love it not! these things are less to me
Than the thin foam that frets upon the sea,
Less than the thistledown of summer air
Which hath no seed: better to stand aloof
Far from these slanderous fools who mock my life
Knowing me not, better the lowliest roof
Fit for the meanest hind to sojourn in,
Than to go back to that hoarse cave of strife
Where my white soul first kissed the mouth of sin.

FROM HUMANITAD

Ah! it was easy when the world was young
   To keep one's life free and inviolate,
From our sad lips another song is rung,
   By our hands our heads are desecrate,
Wanderers in drear exile, and dispossessed
Of what should be our own, we can but feed on wild
    unrest.

Somehow, the grace, the bloom of things has flown,
   And of all men we are most wretched who
Must live each other's lives and not our own
   For very pity's sake and then undo
All that we lived for – it was otherwise
When soul and body seemed to blend in mystic
    symphonies.

But we have left those gentle haunts to pass
   With weary feet to the new Calvary,
Where we behold, as one who in a glass
   Sees his own face, self-slain Humanity,
And in the dumb reproach of that sad gaze
Learn what an awful phantom the red hand of man
    can raise.

O smitten mouth! O forehead crowned with thorn!
    O chalice of all common miseries!
Thou for our sakes that loved thee not hast borne
    An agony of endless centuries,
And we were vain and ignorant nor knew
That when we stabbed thy heart it was our own real
        hearts we slew.

Being ourselves the sowers and the seeds,
    The night that covers and the lights that fade,
The spear that pierces and the side that bleeds,
    The lips betraying and the life betrayed;
The deep hath calm: the moon hath rest: but we
Lords of the natural world are yet our own dread
        enemy.

Is this the end of all primal force
    Which, in its changes being still the same,
From eyeless Chaos cleft its upward course,
    Through ravenous seas and whirling rocks and
        flame,
Till the suns met in heaven and began
Their cycles, and the morning stars sang, and the
    Word was Man!

Nay, nay, we are crucified, and though
   The bloody sweat falls from our brows like rain,
Loosen the nails – we shall come down I know,
   Staunch the red wounds – we shall be whole again,
No need have we of hyssop-laden rod,
That which is purely human, that is Godlike, that is
    God.

THE BALLAD OF READING GAOL

1

He did not wear his scarlet coat,
　For blood and wine are red,
And blood and wine were on his hands
　When they found him with the dead,
The poor dead woman whom he loved,
　And murdered in her bed.

He walked amongst the Trial Men
　In a suit of shabby grey;
A cricket cap was on his head,
　And his step seemed light and gay;
But I never saw a man who looked
　So wistfully at the day.

I never saw a man who looked
　With such a wistful eye
Upon that little tent of blue
　Which prisoners call the sky,
And at every drifting cloud that went
　With sails of silver by.

I walked, with other souls in pain,
　Within another ring,
And was wondering if the man had done
　A great or little thing,
When a voice behind me whispered low,
　'That fellow's got to swing.'

Dear Christ! the very prison walls
  Suddenly seemed to reel,
And the sky above my head became
  Like a casque of scorching steel;
And, though I was a soul in pain,
  My pain I could not feel.

I only knew what hunted thought
  Quickened his step, and why
He looked upon the garish day
  With such a wistful eye;
The man had killed the thing he loved,
  And so he had to die.

Yet each man kills the thing he loves,
  By each let this be heard,
Some do it with a bitter look,
  Some with a flattering word.
The coward does it with a kiss,
  The brave man with a sword!

Some kill their love when they are young,
  And some when they are old;
Some strangle with the hands of Lust,
  Some with the hands of Gold:
The kindest use a knife, because
  The dead so soon grow cold.

Some love too little, some too long,
　　Some sell, and others buy;
Some do the deed with many tears,
　　And some without a sigh:
For each man kills the thing he loves,
　　Yet each man does not die.

He does not die a death of shame
　　On a day of dark disgrace,
Nor have a noose about his neck,
　　Nor a cloth upon his face,
Nor drop feet foremost through the floor
　　Into an empty space.

He does not sit with silent men
　　Who watch him night and day;
Who watch him when he tries to weep,
　　And when he tries to pray;
Who watch him lest himself should rob
　　The prison of its prey.

He does not wake at dawn to see
　　Dread figures throng his room,
The shivering Chaplain robed in white,
　　The Sheriff stern with gloom,
And the Governor all in shiny black,
　　With the yellow face of Doom.

He does not rise in piteous haste
   To put on convict-clothes,
While some coarse-mouthed Doctor gloats,
   and notes
   Each new and nerve-twitched pose,
Fingering a watch whose little ticks
   Are like horrible hammer-blows.

He does not feel that sickening thirst
   That sands one's throat, before
The hangman with his gardener's gloves
   Comes through the padded door,
And binds one with three leathern thongs,
   That the throat may thirst no more.

He does not bend his head to hear
   The Burial Office read,
Nor, while the anguish of his soul
   Tells him he is not dead,
Cross his own coffin, as he moves
   Into the hideous shed.

He does not stare upon the air
   Through a little roof of glass:
He does not pray with lips of clay
   For his agony to pass;
Nor feel upon his shuddering cheek
   The kiss of Caiaphas.

2

Six weeks the guardsman walked the yard,
  In the suit of shabby grey:
His cricket cap was on his head,
  And his step seemed light and gay,
But I never saw a man who looked
  So wistfully at the day.

I never saw a man who looked
  With such a wistful eye
Upon that little tent of blue
  which prisoners call the sky,
And at every wandering cloud that trailed
  Its ravelled fleeces by.

He did not wring his hands, as do
  Those witless men who dare
To try to rear the changeling Hope
  In the cave of black Despair:
He only looked upon the sun,
  And drank the morning air.

He did not wring his hands nor weep,
  Nor did he peek or pine,
But he drank the air as though it held
  Some healthful anodyne;
With open mouth he drank the sun
  As though it had been wine!

And I and all the souls in pain,
   Who tramped the other ring,
Forgot if we ourselves had done
   A great or little thing,
And watched with gaze of dull amaze
   The man who had to swing.

For strange it was to see him pass
   With a step so light and gay,
And strange it was to see him look
   So wistfully at the day,
And strange it was to think that he
   Had such a debt to pay.

For oak and elm have pleasant leaves
   That in the spring-time shoot;
But grim to see is the gallows-tree,
   With its adder-bitten root,
And, green or dry, a man must die
   Before it bears its fruit!

The loftiest place is that seat of grace
   For which all worldlings try:
But who would stand in hempen band
   Upon a scaffold high,
And through a murderer's collar take
   His last look at the sky?

It is sweet to dance to violins
  When Love and Life are fair:
To dance to flutes, to dance to lutes
  Is delicate and rare:
But it is not sweet with nimble feet
  To dance upon the air!

So with curious eyes and sick surmise
  We watched him day by day,
And wondered if each one of us
  Would end the self-same way,
For none can tell to what red Hell
  His sightless soul may stray.

At last the dead man walked no more
  Amongst the Trial Men,
And I knew that he was standing up
  In the black dock's dreadful pen,
And that never would I see his face
  For weal or woe again.

Like two doomed ships that pass in storm
  We had crossed each other's way:
But we made no sign, we said no word,
  We had no word to say;
For we did not meet in the holy night,
  But in the shameful day.

A prison wall was round us both,
   Two outcast men we were:
The world had thrust us from its heart,
   And God from out His care:
And the iron gin that waits for Sin
   Had caught us in its snare.

3

In Debtor's Yard the stones are hard,
   And the dripping wall is high,
So it was there he took the air
   Beneath the leaden sky,
And by each side a Warder walked,
   For fear the man might die.

Or else he sat with those who watched
   His anguish night and day;
Who watched him when he rose to weep,
   And when he crouched to pray;
Who watched him lest himself should rob
   Their scaffold of its prey.

The Governor was strong upon
   The Regulations Act:
The Doctor said that Death was but
   A scientific fact:
And twice a day the Chaplain called,
   And left a little tract.

And twice a day he smoked his pipe,
   And drank his quart of beer:
His soul was resolute, and held
   No hiding-place for fear;
He often said that he was glad
   The hangman's day was near.

But why he said so strange a thing
   No warder dared to ask:
For he to whom a watcher's doom
   Is given as his task,
Must set a lock upon his lips
   And make his face a mask.

Or else he might be moved, and try
   To comfort or console:
And what should Human Pity do
   Pent up in Murderer's Hole?
What word of grace in such a place
   Could help a brother's soul?

With slouch and swing around the ring
   We trod the Fools' Parade!
We did not care: we knew we were
   The Devil's Own Brigade:
And shaven head and feet of lead
   Make a merry masquerade.

We tore the tarry rope to shreds
  With blunt and bleeding nails;
We rubbed the doors, and scrubbed the
    floors,
  And cleaned the shining rails:
And, rank by rank, we soaped the plank,
  And clattered with the pails.

We sewed the sacks, we broke the stones,
  We turned the dusty drill:
We banged the tins, and bawled the hymns,
  And sweated on the mill
But in the heart of every man
  Terror was lying still.

So still it lay that every day
  Crawled like a weed-clogged wave:
And we forgot the bitter lot
  That waits for fool and knave,
Till once, as we tramped in from work,
  We passed an open grave.

With yawning mouth the yellow hole
  Gaped for a living thing;
The very mud cried out for blood
  To the thirsty asphalte ring:
And we knew that ere one dawn grew fair
  Some prisoner had to swing.

Right in we went, with soul intent
   On Death and Dread and Doom:
The hangman, with his little bag,
   Went shuffling through the gloom:
And I trembled as I groped my way
   Into my numbered tomb.

That night the empty corridors
   Were full of forms of Fear,
And up and down the iron town
   Stole feet we could not hear,
And through the bars that hide the stars
   White faces seemed to peer.

He lay as one who lies and dreams
   In a pleasant meadow-land,
The watchers watched him as he slept,
   And could not understand
How one could sleep so sweet a sleep
   With a hangman close at hand.

But there is no sleep when men must weep
   Who never yet have wept:
So we - the fool, the fraud, the knave—
   That endless vigil kept,
And through each brain on hands of pain
   Another's terror crept.

Alas! it is a fearful thing
   To feel another's guilt!
For, right, within, the Sword of Sin
   Pierced to its poisoned hilt,
And as molten lead were the tears we shed
   For the blood we had not spilt.

The warders with their shoes of felt
   Crept by each padlocked door,
And peeped and saw, with eyes of awe,
   Grey figures on the floor,
And wondered why men knelt to pray
   Who never prayed before.

All through the night we knelt and prayed,
   Mad mourners of a corse!
The troubled plumes of midnight shook
   The plumes upon a hearse:
And bitter wine upon a sponge
   Was the savour of Remorse.

The grey cock crew, the red cock crew,
   But never came the day:
And crooked shapes of Terror crouched,
   In the corners where we lay:
And each evil sprite that walks by night
   Before us seemed to play.

They glided past, they glided fast,
　　Like travellers through a mist:
They mocked the moon in a rigadoon
　　Of delicate turn and twist,
And with formal pace and loathsome grace
　　The phantoms kept their tryst.

With mop and mow, we saw them go,
　　Slim shadows hand in hand:
About, about, in ghostly rout
　　They trod a saraband:
And the damned grotesques made
　　　arabesques,
　　Like the wind upon the sand!

With the pirouettes of marionettes,
　　They tripped on pointed tread:
But with flutes of Fear they filled the ear,
　　As their grisly masque they led,
And loud they sang, and long they sang,
　　For they sang to wake the dead.

'Oho!' they cried, 'The world is wide,
　　But fettered limbs go lame!
And once, or twice, to throw the dice
　　Is a gentlemanly game,
But he does not win who plays with Sin
　　In the secret House of Shame.'

No things of air these antics were,
    That frolicked with such glee:
To men whose lives were held in gyves,
    And whose feet might not go free,
Ah! wounds of Christ! they were living things
    Most terrible to see.

Around, around, they waltzed and wound;
    Some wheeled in smirking pairs;
With the mincing step of a demirep
    Some sidled up the stairs;
And with subtle sneer, and fawning leer,
    Each helped us at our prayers.

The morning wind began to moan,
    But still the night went on:
Through its giant loom the web of gloom
    Crept till each thread was spun:
And, as we prayed, we grew afraid
    Of the Justice of the Sun.

The moaning wind went wandering round
    The weeping prison-wall:
Till like a wheel of turning steel
    We felt the minutes crawl:
O moaning wind! what had we done
    To have such a seneschal?

At last I saw the shadowed bars,
  Like a lattice wrought in lead,
Move right across the whitewashed wall
  That faced my three-plank bed,
And I knew that somewhere in the world
  God's dreadful dawn was red.

At six o'clock we cleaned our cells,
  At seven all was still
But the sough and swing of a mighty wing
  The prison seemed to fill,
For the Lord of Death with icy breath
  Had entered in to kill.

He did not pass in purple pomp,
  Nor ride a moon-white steed.
Three yards of cord and a sliding board
  Are all the gallows' need:
So with rope of shame the Herald came
  To do the secret deed.

We were as men who through a fen
  Of filthy darkness grope:
We did not dare to breathe a prayer,
  Or to give our anguish scope:
Something was dead in each of us,
  And what was dead was Hope.

For Man's grim Justice goes its way,
    And will not swerve aside:
It slays the weak, it slays the strong,
    It has a deadly stride:
With iron heel it slays the strong,
    The monstrous parricide!

We waited for the stroke of eight:
    Each tongue was thick with thirst:
For the stroke of eight is the stroke of Fate
    That makes a man accursed,
And Fate will use a running noose
    For the best man and the worst.

We had no other thing to do,
    Save to wait for the sign to come:
So, like things of stone in a valley lone,
    Quiet we sat and dumb:
But each man's heart beat thick and quick,
    Like a madman on a drum!

With a sudden shock the prison-clock
    Smote on the shivering air,
And from all the gaol rose up a wail
    Of impotent despair,
Like the sound that frightened marches hear
    From some leper in his lair.

And as one sees most fearful things
   In the crystal of a dream,
We saw the greasy hempen rope
   Hooked to the blackened beam,
And heard the prayer the hangman's snare
   Strangled into a scream.

And all the woe that moved him so
   That he gave that bitter cry,
And the wild regrets, and the bloody sweats,
   None knew so well as I:
For he who lives more lives than one
   More deaths than one must die.

4

There is no chapel on the day
   On which they hang a man:
The Chaplain's heart is far too sick,
   Or his face is far too wan,
Or there is that written in his eyes
   Which none should look upon.

So they kept us close till nigh on noon,
   And then they rang the bell,
And the warders with their jingling keys
   Opened each listening cell,
And down the iron stair we tramped,
   Each from his separate Hell.

Out into God's sweet air we went,
    But not in wonted way,
For this man's face was white with fear,
    And that man's face was grey,
And I never saw sad men who looked
    So wistfully at the day.

I never saw sad men who looked
    With such a wistful eye
Upon that little tent of blue
    We prisoners called the sky,
And at every happy cloud that passed
    In such strange freedom by.

But there were those amongst us all
    Who walked with downcast head,
And knew that, had each got his due,
    They should have died instead:
He had but killed a thing that lived,
    Whilst they had killed the dead.

For he who sins a second time
    Wakes a dead soul to pain,
And draws it from its spotted shroud,
    And makes it bleed again,
And makes it bleed great gouts of blood,
    And makes it bleed in vain!

Like ape or clown, in monstrous garb
    With crooked arrows starred,
Silently we went round and round
    The slippery asphalte yard;
Silently we went round and round,
    And no man spoke a word.

Silently we went round and round,
    And through each hollow mind
The Memory of dreadful things
    Rushed like a dreadful wind,
And Horror stalked before each man,
    And Terror crept behind.

The warders strutted up and down,
    And watched their herd of brutes,
Their uniforms were spick and span,
    And they wore their Sunday suits,
But we knew the work they had been at,
    By the quicklime on their boots.

For where a grave had opened wide,
    There was no grave at all:
Only a stretch of mud and sand
    By the hideous prison-wall,
And a little heap of burning lime,
    That the man should have his pall.

For he has a pall, this wretched man,
    Such as few men can claim:
Deep down below a prison-yard,
    Naked for greater shame,
He lies, with fetters on each foot,
    Wrapt in a sheet of flame!

And all the while the burning lime
    Eats flesh and bone away,
It eats the brittle bone by night,
    And the soft flesh by day,
It eats the flesh and bone by turns,
    But it eats the heart alway.

For three long years they will not sow
    Or root or seedling there:
For three long years the unblessed spot
    Will sterile be and bare,
And look upon the wondering sky
    With unreproachful stare.

They think a murderer's heart would taint
    Each simple seed they sow.
It is not true! God's kindly earth
    Is kindlier than men know,
And the red rose would but blow more red,
    The white rose whiter blow.

Out of his mouth a red, red rose!
    Out of his heart a white!
For who can say by what strange way,
    Christ brings His will to light,
Since the barren staff the pilgrim bore
    Bloomed in the great Pope's sight?

But neither milk-white rose nor red
    May bloom in prison-air;
The shard, the pebble, and the flint,
    Are what they give us there:
For flowers have been known to heal
    A common man's despair.

So never will wine-red rose or white,
    Petal by petal, fall
On that stretch of mud and sand that lies
    By the hideous prison-wall,
To tell the men who tramp the yard
    That God's Son died for all.

Yet though the hideous prison-wall
    Still hems him round and round,
And a spirit may not walk by night
    That is with fetters bound,
And a spirit may but weep that lies
    In such unholy ground,

He is at peace – this wretched man—
    At peace, or will be soon:
There is no thing to make him mad,
    Nor does Terror walk at noon,
For the lampless Earth in which he lies
    Has neither Sun nor Moom.

They hanged him as a beast is hanged!
    They did now even toll
A requiem that might have brought
    Rest to his startled soul,
But hurriedly they took him out,
    And hid him in a hole.

The warders stripped him of his clothes,
    And gave him to the flies:
They mocked the swollen purple throat,
    And the stark and staring eyes:
And with laughter loud they heaped the
        shroud
    In which the convict lies.

The Chaplain would not kneel to pray
    By his dishonoured grave:
Nor mark it with that blessed Cross
    That Christ for sinners gave,
Because the man was one of those
    Whom Christ came down to save.

Yet all is well; he has but passed
   To Life's appointed bourne:
And alien tears will fill for him
   Pity's long-broken urn,
For his mourners will be outcast men,
   And outcasts always mourn.

5

I know not whether Laws be right,
   Or whether Laws be wrong;
All that we know who lie in gaol
   Is that the wall is strong;
And that each day is like a year,
   A year whose days are long.

But this I know, that every Law
   That men hath made for Man,
Since first Man took his brother's life,
   And the sad world began,
But straws the wheat and saves the chaff
   With a most evil fan.

This too I know – and wise it were
   If each could know the same—
That every prison that men build
   Is built with bricks of shame,
And bound with bars lest Christ should see
   How men their brothers maim.

With bars they blur the gracious moon,
   And blind the goodly sun;
And they do well to hide their Hell,
   For in it things are done
That Son of God nor son of Man
   Ever should look upon!

The vilest deeds like poison weeds,
   Bloom well in prison-air;
It is only what is good in Man
   That wastes and withers there:
Pale Anguish keeps the heavy gate,
   And the Warder is Despair.

For they starve the little frightened child
   Till it weeps both night and day:
And they scourge the weak, and flog the fool,
   And gibe the old and grey,
And some grow mad, and all grow bad,
   And none a word may say.

Each narrow cell in which we dwell
   Is a foul and dark latrine,
And the fetid breath of living Death
   Chokes up each grated screen,
And all, but Lust, is turned to dust
   In Humanity's machine.

The brackish water that we drink
   Creeps with a loathsome slime,
And the bitter bread they weigh in scales
   Is full of chalk and lime,
And Sleep will not lie down, but walks
   Wild-eyed, and cries to Time.

But though lean Hunger and green Thirst
   Like asp with adder fight,
We have little care of prison fare,
   For what chills and kills outright
Is that every stone one lifts by day
   Becomes one's heart by night.

With midnight always in one's heart,
   And twilight in one's cell,
We turn the crank, or tear the rope,
   Each in his separate Hell,
And the silence is more awful far
   Than the sound of a brazen bell.

And never a human voice comes near
   To speak a gentle word:
And the eye that watches through the door
   Is pitiless and hard:
And by all forgot, we rot and rot,
   With soul and body marred.

And thus we rust Life's iron chain
   Degraded and alone:
And some men curse, and some men weep,
   And some men make no moan:
But God's eternal Laws are kind
   And break the heart of stone.

And every human heart that breaks,
   In prison-cell or yard,
Is as that broken box that gave
   Its treasure to the Lord,
And filled the unclean leper's house
   With the scent of costliest nard.

Ah! happy they whose hearts can break
   And peace of pardon win!
How else may man make straight his plan
   And cleanse his soul from Sin?
How else but through a broken heart
   May Lord Christ enter in?

And he of the swollen purple throat,
   And the stark and staring eyes,
Waits for the holy hands that took
   The Thief to Paradise;
And a broken and a contrite heart
   The Lord will not despise.

The man in red who reads the Law
   Gave him three weeks of life,
Three little weeks in which to heal
   His soul of his soul's strife,
And cleanse from every blot of blood
   The hand that held the knife.

And with tears of blood he cleansed the
     hand,
   The hand that held the steel:
For only blood can wipe out blood,
   And only tears can heal:
And the crimson stain that was of Cain
   Became Christ's snow-white seal.

6

In Reading gaol by Reading town
   There is a pit of shame,
And in it lies a wretched man
   Eaten by teeth of flame,
In a burning winding-sheet he lies,
   And his grave has got no name.

And there, till Christ call forth the dead,
   In silence let him lie:
No need to waste the foolish tear,
   Or heave the windy sigh:
The man had killed the thing he loved,
   And so he had to die.